THE OFFICIAL
ENGLAND RUGBY
ANNUAL 2015

Written by Iain Spragg

Designed by Brian Thomson

A Grange Publication

©2014. Published by Grange Communications Ltd., Edinburgh, under licence from the RFU. The England Rose, word England Rugby and Ruckley are official registered trademarks of the Rugby Football Union and are the subjects of extensive trademark registrations worldwide. The Gilbert logo and trim is a registered trademark of Gilbert Rugby. Printed in the EU.

Photographs © RFU via Getty Images and Action Images.

ISBN: 978-1-908925-77-0

10654128

CONTENTS

WELCOME TO THE OFFICIAL ENGLAND RUGBY

ANNUAL 2015

This year's Annual is our best ever with a bumper collection of fantastic features and the lowdown on all the star players to keep even the biggest England rugby fan happy.

Stuart Lancaster's exciting young England team produced some brilliant performances in 2014 and we've got a round-up of all the big games as the marvellous men in white won the Triple Crown for the first time in 10 years and continued their impressive build-up for the World Cup on home soil in 2015.

We've got a review of a superb Six Nations season for the England Women's team, as well as all the news on the England Under 20s defence of their IRB Junior World Championship title in New Zealand and how the Sevens side performed in the explosive and popular World Sevens Series.

There are fabulous features on the England internationals who shone in 2014 and we also take a look at some of the younger players we think will become stars of the team in the future.

And if you fancy yourself as an England rugby trivia champion, there's our fiendish quiz, 'Spot The Ball' and 'Guess Who?' pages to test your knowledge on Lancaster's team.

We hope you enjoy this year's Annual!

Danny Care 46th Cap 1301

RBS 6 NATIONS 2014 ROUND-UP

Stuart Lancaster's third Six Nations campaign as head coach was the best yet as his exciting England team claimed the Triple Crown for the first time since 2003 after wins over Scotland, Ireland and Wales.

The dream of a famous Grand Slam came to an end after the side were beaten in the dying minutes of their opening game against France in Paris, but England bounced back brilliantly to win their next four games and finish second in the Championship table.

The defeat in France was a bitter disappointment but England's young players proved the future is bright with some great attacking performances. They scored 14 Championship tries in the process – the team's best tally in the tournament for five years.

Even better news for Lancaster were the individual displays of new boys Luther Burrell, Jack Nowell and George Ford, who all made their debuts during the tournament, as well as the superb captaincy of Chris Robshaw and the dazzling form of full back Mike Brown, who was voted the 2014 Six Nations Player of the Year.

England will want to go one better in 2015 but Lancaster can look back on 2014 as another important step in the right direction.

Week One

France 26 England 24

England had won three of their last four matches in Paris but made a bad start in the Stade de France as home winger Yoann Huget scored two tries in the first 17 minutes to put the team firmly on the back foot.

Other sides might have crumbled under the fierce French onslaught but England showed real character and just four minutes before half-time they scored a great try through Brown after a clever break by Danny Care. After the break Burrell scored on his debut and, when Farrell converted, England were in front for the first time in the match.

A penalty for each side saw Lancaster's team sitting on a team lead 24-19 but just four minutes before the final whistle disaster struck when France launched a desperate attack from the half way line. England's defence raced across to stop the danger but they ran out of tacklers and substitute Gael Fickou scored beneath the posts. The conversion made it 26-24 to the home side and England were beaten.

"The positives outweigh the negatives but we know we must improve to win the big games," said Lancaster after the game. "I thought the boys showed incredible character, resilience and a lot of skill to put us in a position to win."

Week Two

Scotland 0 England 20

Despite the heartbreak of the last-gasp loss in Paris, Lancaster picked the same starting 15 to face Scotland at Murrayfield seven days later and the team didn't let him down as they cruised to an easy victory in Edinburgh.

The powerful England forwards were in charge throughout the match but it was scrum half Care who began the scoring in the fifth minute with a cheeky drop goal. The first of England's two tries came nine minutes later when Burrell scored for a second Test match in a row after the Northampton centre had burst through the Scottish midfield and at half-time the team were 13-0 up.

Lancaster's side looked more and more dangerous in the second half and it was the impressive Brown who added the second try after a strong break from Nowell down the blindside. Farrell added the conversion and the score was 20-0 to the visitors.

England were unable to add any more tries at Murrayfield. It was the first time they had stopped the opposition scoring any points since they demolished Canada 70-0 at Twickenham 10 years earlier.

Week Three

England 13 Ireland 10

England were looking for a fourth win on the bounce against Ireland and after an epic game in front of 82,000 fans at Twickenham, that's exactly what they achieved.

A Farrell penalty after 24 minutes was the only score of a tense but entertaining first half but Ireland came storming back just after the restart when full back Rob Kearney sliced open the defence for the first try. Jonny Sexton landed the conversion and the visitors had their noses in front.

England needed a moment of magic to get back into the match and it was Brown and then Care who provided it. Brown made the initial break from halfway and just as the Ireland players closed him down, Care was on hand to take a perfect pass and sprint underneath the posts.

It was the last score of the game and when the whistle went for full time, England were able to celebrate an important 13-10 win.

"The lads were outstanding," said Man-of-the-Match Brown. "We were pretty happy at half-time but we needed to finish off the phases. Ireland were unbeaten and we wanted to set a marker."

"The lads were outstanding"

Week Four

England 29 Wales 18

Grand Slam champions Wales arrived at Twickenham two weeks later hoping to deny England the Triple Crown but the men in white had not forgotten the disappointment of their heavy 30-3 defeat in Cardiff a year earlier and took their revenge with a convincing win.

Care settled the nerves in the fifth minute when he took a quick tap penalty that caught the Welsh defence napping and the scrum half was able to dive over the try line completely unopposed.

Much of the match was a battle between the boots of Farrell and Wales full back Leigh Halfpenny, who landed 11 penalties between them, but it was that man Burrell who supplied England's crucial second try.

England were on the attack when Billy Twelvetrees opted for a clever grubber kick behind the Irish defence and it was Burrell who was quickest to react, pouncing on the bouncing ball for his third try of the tournament.

"I was really proud of the team," Lancaster said after the final whistle. "They are a great set of lads who always want to play hard for each other and the shirt. It's nice to get the win to put last year's result in Cardiff to bed. We lost fair and square on that day but this was our day and we deserved to win."

Week Five

Italy 11 England 52

England needed France to beat Ireland in Paris to stand a realistic chance of topping the Six Nations table but the first job was beating Italy, a task they completed in spectacular style with a seven-try romp in Rome.

England's attacking play was superb in the Italian capital as Brown helped himself to his third and then fourth tries of the tournament in the first half and there was also a score for Farrell before the break.

The tries continued to flow after the restart, with Manu Tuilagi and Robshaw both going over, while there were also first international scores for Nowell and Mako Vunipola as Lancaster's side recorded a half century of points.

Sadly, it was not enough to win the Championship thanks to Ireland's narrow 22-20 victory in France a few hours later but England could still look back on a successful campaign with plenty of positives.

"The response after France has been outstanding," said captain Robshaw. "We always knew it was going to be tough. We came here to score 50 points and that's what we did."

> "We came here to score 50 points and that's what we did"

FINAL TABLE

	W	D	L	T	F	A	Pts
Ireland	4	0	1	16	132	49	8
England	4	0	1	14	138	65	8
Wales	3	0	2	11	122	79	6
France	3	0	2	9	101	100	6
Scotland	1	0	4	4	47	138	2
Italy	0	0	5	7	63	172	0

TWICKENHAM
IN NUMBƐR5

Everything you need to know about the world famous home of the England rugby team.

10 The number of games the stadium will host during the 2015 World Cup, including the final on 31st October.

82,000 The maximum capacity of Twickenham on match days, making it the biggest stadium devoted to rugby in the world.

156 The number of rooms at the London Marriott, the hotel in the stadium's South Stand.

2 The number of internationals at Twickenham that have had to be postponed because of bad weather. The first was the Test against France in 1947, the second the match against Scotland in 1987.

220,000 The amount in pounds spent by supporters at the Rugby Store on international match days.

5,572 The amount in pounds the RFU paid in 1907 for the farm land in southwest London on which they built the stadium.

20 The most tries recorded by an England side at the ground in a Test, scored in the 134-0 defeat of Romania in 2001.

18,000 The number of fans who watched the first ever international at Twickenham, the match between England and Wales in 1910.

95,971 The number of fans who squeezed into the stadium to watch Rihanna on her Diamonds World Tour in 2013.

15 The number of different countries who have played England at Twickenham. They are Scotland, Ireland, Wales, France, Italy, New Zealand, Australia, South Africa, Argentina, Romania, USA, Fiji, Canada, Samoa and Tonga.

10,500 The number of meals served inside the stadium on international match days.

669 The total number of tries England had scored in 279 internationals at the stadium by the end of the 2014 Six Nations.

22 England's longest winning streak at Twickenham. It began with a 101-10 defeat of Tonga in October 1999 and after 21 more wins, finally came to an end in September 2003 when Ireland won 19-13 in London.

10,000 The number of exhibits on show in the stadium's World Rugby Museum.

1.5 The amount in millions of pounds the RFU spent in 2012 installing the ground's state-of-the-art Desso pitch, a tough mix of natural grass and artificial fibres.

105 The length of the Twickenham pitch in metres. It is 69 metres wide.

1 The number of games England lost in their first 20 games at HQ – a 9-3 defeat to South Africa in January 1913.

37 The number of Championship games staged at the stadium since the start of the Six Nations in 2000.

MEET THE BOSS

Stuart Lancaster has worked wonders with the England squad since becoming the new head coach in 2011.

When England crashed out of the World Cup that was held in New Zealand in 2011, losing to France in the quarter-finals, it was time for the RFU to find a new coach. They turned to Stuart Lancaster and since getting the job he has transformed England into one of the best teams in the world.

A former flanker who actually played for Scotland at Under 21 level, the man from Cumbria began his coaching as a school teacher. He joined Leeds Carnegie as academy manager before being appointed Director of Rugby. Lancaster then joined the RFU as Head of Elite Player Development and was England Saxon's Head Coach.

In 2011 he led the England Saxons team to victory in the Churchill Cup and just a few months later he was asked to revive the senior England team's fortunes after their World Cup disappointment.

He got the job on a temporary basis at first but after some impressive performances from his side during the 2012 Six Nations, he was named permanent head coach. Since then England have gotten better and better.

Lancaster believes in hard work, team spirit and modesty from his players and his approach to coaching has seen England rise steadily up the International Rugby Board world rankings in the last three years, as well as claiming famous victories over the All Blacks and the Wallabies at Twickenham.

During his reign, Lancaster has never been afraid to give young players a first chance in international rugby and thanks to his ability to spot new talent, England look in great shape to challenge for the 2015 World Cup.

THE LANCASTER FACTFILE

Date of Birth: 9 October, 1969

Place of Birth: Penrith, Cumbria

Playing Career: Wakefield, Leeds

Coaching Career: Leeds, England Saxons, England

England Record*: P27 W18 D1 L8

Six Nations Record*: P12 W9 D0 L0

Up to the end of the 2014 Six Nations

THE BACKROOM BOYS

Meet the coaches helping Stuart Lancaster to plot a course to Rugby World Cup glory in 2015.

ANDY FARRELL, BACKS COACH

A star player in rugby league with Wigan Warriors and later in his career for Saracens in rugby union, Farrell is a key figure in the England set-up and the man in charge of the backs. He switched codes in 2005, winning eight caps for England and playing at the 2007 World Cup in France. After he retired two year later, he became first-team coach at Saracens, winning the Premiership title in 2011. He first got involved with the England team during the 2012 Six Nations and was assistant coach on the British & Irish Lions winning tour of Australia in 2013.

GRAHAM ROWNTREE, FORWARDS COACH

A brilliant prop as a player, Rowntree has been working for the RFU since he was appointed as a National Academy coach in 2007 and is the man responsible for making sure the England forwards are ready for battle. He won 54 caps and two Grand Slams as an England player and also made three Test appearances for the British & Irish Lions against Argentina and the All Blacks in 2005. After joining the RFU Academy, he was promoted to England scrum coach but now has the job of looking after all areas of the pack's play.

MIKE CATT, ATTACKING SKILLS COACH

As one of the most naturally talented players of his generation, it's no surprise Catt is now coaching the current group of England stars and helping to improve their attacking skills. He was part of the England team that famously won the 2003 World Cup in Sydney and he played international rugby for 13 years before finally hanging up his boots. His coaching career began in 2008 at London Irish, where he was attack coach and in 2012 he joined the England set-up ahead of the summer tour to South Africa.

In The Spotlight

Luther Burrell

After making an explosive start to his England career in the 2014 Six Nations, the Northampton Saints centre has become one of the most deadly finishers in Stuart Lancaster's young side.

There aren't many players who can say they scored a try on their Test debut but Luther Burrell can, after he raced over for a brilliant second-half score against France in Paris in the 2014 Six Nations in his first ever appearance for England.

His dream start to his international rugby career continued a week later when he scored again in a dominant 20-0 victory over Scotland at Murrayfield and the Saints star made it a hat-trick of tries in just four games for his county when he crossed the line as Wales were beaten 29-18 at Twickenham and England claimed the Triple Crown.

Powerfully built but lightning quick, Burrell played rugby league as a teenager for the Huddersfield Giants club but was inspired to switch codes and play the 15-a-side game after watching England legends like Jonny Wilkinson and Jason Robinson in international action.

He joined Leeds Carnegie in 2006 and after five seasons in Yorkshire and one year with the Sale Sharks, he signed for Northampton in 2012.

His arrival at Franklin's Gardens saw Burrell make a real name for himself in the Premiership with his ability to burst through tight defences and although he hadn't progressed through the junior England ranks like many of Lancaster's current squad, it was only a matter of time before he won his first senior cap.

Burrell's amazing performances for England came as no surprise to Saints fans. The centre was in fantastic form for the club in the 2013-14 season and he was a key part of the Northampton team that beat Bath in the final of the European Challenge Cup and then toppled Saracens in the Premiership final at Twickenham to claim a famous double for the club.

THAT'S A FACT!

The Northampton star got his big break as a teenager when his mum emailed Stuart Lancaster to demand he give Luther a trial at the Leeds Academy.

England Rugby

OWEN FARRELL

20

RECORD BREAKERS

The England players who've made history wearing the famous white shirt

CAP MILESTONE

Prop Jason Leonard clocked up a record 114 games for England during a remarkable international career that lasted 14 years. He was part of the team that won the World Cup in 2003 and also played five Tests for the British & Irish Lions.

POINTS MACHINE

No-one has scored more points for England than Jonny Wilkinson. The fly half amassed 1179 points in 91 games for his country and if you include the 67 points he scored for the British & Irish Lions in six appearances, his international career total is 1246.

YOUNG GUN

Fly half Colin Laird was just 18 years and 134 days old when he made his debut against Wales in 1927, making him the youngest ever England player.

HODGSON THE HERO

The record for the most points scored in a Test match belongs to fly half Charlie Hodgson, who registered an incredible 44 points on his international debut against Romania in 2001. England won the game 134-0 as the number 10 notched up two tries, 14 conversions and two penalties.

SUPREME FINISHER

Wing Rory Underwood is England's all-time leading try scorer with 49 in 85 games. The speedster scored five tries in the 58-23 win over Fiji at Twickenham in 1989.

OLD TIMER

The oldest man ever to pull on the white shirt of England was Frederick Gilbert, who was 38 years and 362 days old when he made his debut against Wales in 1923. The full back won just two caps.

CAPTAIN FANTASTIC

Leading England is a huge honour and centre Will Carling holds the record for the most games as skipper with 59. He was first handed the captaincy against Australia at Twickenham in 1988 while his last game in charge was against Ireland eight years later. The team won 44 times while he was captain.

LOYAL SERVANT

Leonard might have the most caps but second rower Simon Shaw boasts the longest England career. The lock was first capped against Italy in 1996 and made his final international appearance 15 years later against France in the World Cup.

WORLD CUP COUNTDOWN

With England hosting rugby's biggest tournament in 2015, fans can look forward to watching the game's greatest players and most exciting teams in action at a stadium near you soon.

The battle to be crowned world champions will begin at Twickenham on 18th September 2015 when England kick off their bid for the Webb Ellis Cup. Over the next six weeks the game's top 20 teams will be battling for the silverware.

England will be hoping to win the competition for a second time after beating Australia in the World Cup final in 2003 thanks to Jonny Wilkinson's famous injury-time drop goal, but defending champions New Zealand won't give up their title without a fight.

THE WORLD CUP VENUES

Twickenham (London)

Olympic Stadium (London)

Millennium Stadium (Cardiff)

Wembley Stadium (London)

Etihad Stadium (Manchester)

Brighton Community Stadium

Elland Road (Leeds)

Kingsholm Stadium (Gloucester)

Leicester City Stadium

Sandy Park (Exeter)

St James' Park (Newcastle)

Stadium MK (Milton Keynes)

Villa Park (Birmingham)

WORLD CUP CHAMPIONS

1987	New Zealand
1991	Australia
1995	South Africa
1999	Australia
2003	ENGLAND
2007	South Africa
2011	New Zealand

The competition is a massive event and with teams like Tonga and the USA, Japan and Samoa having qualified alongside big guns like Australia and South Africa, there will be sides from all over the world to watch and enjoy.

The 2015 World Cup will be the third time England has staged matches in the finals and with hundreds of thousands going to the games and millions more around the globe watching on television, the tournament is set to be the biggest and best ever.

A total of 13 grounds, including St James' Park in Newcastle and the Brighton Community Stadium on the south coast, have been chosen to stage matches in 2015 and when the world's star players all arrive in England, there'll be no shortage of amazing talent on show.

The last time England hosted the World Cup in 1991 the team went all the way to the final and with head coach Stuart Lancaster building an exciting young team to challenge in 2015, hopes are high for another successful tournament.

England are the only northern hemisphere country to have lifted the Webb Ellis Cup after their 1991 triumph and with home advantage in 2015 and the backing of millions of Red Rose supporters, the country is dreaming of glory again.

ISO 64

In The Spotlight

Courtney Lawes

One of the best tacklers in world rugby and an unbelievable natural athlete, the Northampton Saints second rower has become the heartbeat of the powerful England pack.

Courtney Lawes has come a long way since he made his international debut as a 20-year-old substitute against Australia at Twickenham back in 2009. The youngster's talent was never in doubt but his inexperience and injuries meant his early England career was full of highs and lows.

Fast forward to 2014 and the Saints lock is now one of the first names on Stuart Lancaster's team sheet and after a series of stunning performances for England in the 2014 Six Nations, he has matured into one of the best all-round forwards in the game today.

Capped by England at Under 18 and Under 20 level, he also played for the Saxons team before the call came from the senior team and with more than 30 caps under his belt, he's now one of the most experienced and influential players in the England squad. He played three times at the 2011 World Cup in New Zealand and was also part of the team that famously beat the All Blacks at Twickenham in 2012.

His journey to England stardom began when Lawes' family moved from London to Northampton when he was young. It wasn't long before he was playing for local side, the Northampton Old Scouts, and from there he joined the Saints Academy. Since being promoted to the Saints senior side, he has won two European Challenge Cups and the Premiership title in 2014 with the team.

Lawes' top skills are his speed across the pitch, his tackling and his ability to play in the back row as well as in the second row. He's also the man who decides the all-important calls for the England lineout.

THAT'S A FACT!

When he was part of the England Under 20 squad Lawes was nicknamed 'Mr Tickle', after the Mr Men character, because of his extra long arms and legs.

England Rugby

MARLAND YARDE

Ruckley's
Guess Who?

Can you guess who the players are in the pictures below?

Answers on Page 61

STARS OF THE FUTURE
Anthony Watson

A natural athlete with blistering pace, the Bath wing has built a formidable reputation for himself as one of English rugby's deadliest finishers.

Although Anthony Watson doesn't celebrate his 21st birthday until 2015, the youngster is already part of the senior England set-up and was a standout performer for the England Under 20 team that were crowned world champions.

He began his professional career as a teenager when he signed for London Irish, becoming the Exiles' youngest ever first team player, and he's now on the wing as a regular for Bath in the Premiership.

His breakthrough year was in 2013 when he was selected for the Under 20 side to compete at the IRB Junior World Championship in France. Watson played in every game as England lifted the trophy and scored a crucial interception try in the semi-final victory over New Zealand.

He was also part of the England Under 20 side that won the Six Nations in 2013 and more recently he was selected for Stuart Lancaster's senior squad that toured New Zealand, scoring a try in the midweek game against the Crusaders.

Watson, who was nominated for the Premiership Young Player of the Year award in 2014, is equally comfortable on the wing or at full back and is now pushing more senior players like Jonny May and Chris Ashton for a regular place in Lancaster's starting England XV.

Luke Cowan-Dickie

The Exeter Chiefs youngster is one of the new generation of English forwards with a place in Stuart Lancaster's squad firmly in his sights.

Luke Cowan-Dickie is hoping to become a regular Test player much earlier in his career than most. The signs indicate that the dynamic Chiefs hooker is on target to fulfill his dream.

Part of the Exeter Academy set-up, Cowan-Dickie originally played prop but switched to hooker and made his debut for the Chiefs back in 2011 in the European Challenge Cup when was just 18-years-old.

A strong and mobile ball carrier with a fantastic work rate, he has now established himself in the senior Exeter squad. He came off the bench in the Chiefs' famous 15-8 victory over Northampton in the final of the 2014 Anglo-Welsh Cup, the club's first ever major trophy.

An England Under 18 cap and Six Nations winner with the Under 20 squad, Cowan-Dickie was also in the starting England 15 that beat Wales 23-15 in the final of the IRB Junior World Championship in 2013.

He has yet to play for the full England side but his impressive performances in the Premiership were recognised when he was named in Stuart Lancaster's initial 30-man squad to tour New Zealand in the summer.

Henry Slade

A fearless fly half with a box of amazing tricks, the Exeter Chiefs star is aiming to put the pressure on Owen Farrell for the prized England number 10 shirt.

For Slade, a clever tactician and natural leader, the highlight of his career so far came when he was selected to play for England in the non-cap clash with the Barbarians. He marked the occasion with a try and 16 points at HQ.

It's been a busy couple of years for Henry Slade for both club and country. In 2012 he was a talented teenager on the fringes of the Exeter first team, but fast forward to 2014 and he's now a fully-fledged Premiership player who has appeared for England at Twickenham.

His big break came at the end of 2012 when he was handed his Chiefs debut against London Welsh and Slade hasn't looked back since then as he's matured into one of the most exciting English number 10s in the game.

A member of the England team that won the IRB Junior World Championship in France in 2013, scoring 55 points in the tournament, he also starred for the Under 20 side that won the Six Nations title in the same year.

At club level he shone for Exeter in the 2013-14 season, making 18 appearances in the Premiership and kicking a penalty and conversion in victory in the final of the Anglo-Welsh Cup against Northampton.

Semesa Rokoduguni

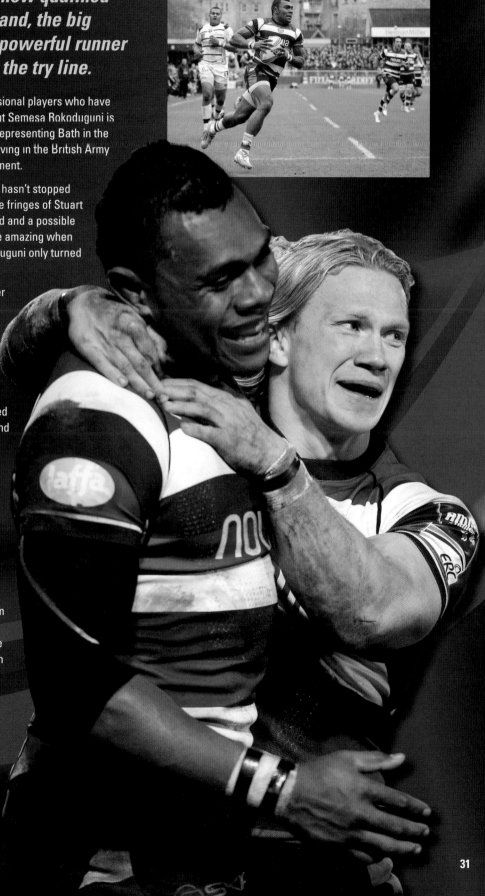

Born in Fiji but now qualified to play for England, the big Bath wing is a powerful runner with an eye for the try line.

There aren't many professional players who have a career outside rugby, but Semesa Rokoduguni is an exception to the rule, representing Bath in the Premiership while still serving in the British Army as a soldier in a tank regiment.

It's an unusual story but it hasn't stopped him working his way to the fringes of Stuart Lancaster's England squad and a possible Test debut. It is even more amazing when you remember that Rokoduguni only turned professional in 2012.

Bath were the club to offer him his big chance and he repaid the club's faith with seven tries in 17 starts in his first two seasons at the Recreation Ground.

His impressive form earned him a call-up to the England Saxons squad in early 2014 and although injury denied him the chance to pull on the famous white jersey for the first time, it wasn't long before he got another shot.

It came in June when Lancaster named his England team to face the Barbarians at Twickenham and Rokoduguni was in the starting XV. Caps were not awarded for the match at HQ but the Bath star had still taken another important step towards full international honours.

In The Spotlight

Danny Care

A twinkle-toed scrum half with an eye for the tryline and a competitive instinct, the Harlequins star was in the best form of his Test career in 2014.

The role of scrum half is one of the most important on the modern rugby pitch and in Danny Care England are lucky to have one of the most talented and clever number nines around today. Care has been part of the England set-up since 2008 but he really came of age in 2014 with a series of superb performances in the Six Nations.

His international career started when he came off the bench against the All Blacks in Auckland. His first start for the team came a week later in Christchurch but for much of his time as an international player he has had to battle with the likes of Harry Ellis, Lee Dickson and Ben Youngs for the number nine spot.

That all changed in this year's Championship when the Quins man made the shirt his own and he repaid Stuart Lancaster's faith in him with two tries and two drop goals during the tournament.

Care started playing when he was just six years old. His first senior club was Otley in Yorkshire but his career really started to take off when he joined Leeds. After he had represented England at every junior level, it was obvious he was destined for stardom.

He now plays in the Premiership for Harlequins and was in the starting 15s for the London club when they won the European Challenge Cup final against Stade Français in 2011 and the Premiership final against Leicester a year later.

The scrum half's speed of thought matches his pace and since forcing his way into the England squad, Care has notched up nearly 50 caps and scored tries in big games against New Zealand, Ireland, South Africa and Wales.

THAT'S A FACT!

Care is a brilliant footballer and was part of the Sheffield Wednesday Academy as a youngster before deciding to concentrate on rugby full time.

ENGLAND WOMEN
CLAIM TRIPLE CROWN

Gary Street's side matched the success of Stuart Lancaster's side in their 2014 Six Nations campaign, beating the three Home Union teams to complete a domestic clean sweep.

After a disappointing Six Nations in 2013, England's women bounced back in style in 2014 with victories over Scotland, Ireland and Wales to claim the Triple Crown for the 16th time in the history of the Championship.

The team also comfortably beat Italy in their final match of the tournament to record a fourth win, but were narrowly denied a Grand Slam after losing to France in Grenoble on the opening weekend of action.

The results meant England finished as runners-up behind the French but after coming third in 2013 – their worst performance since the Championship began in 1996 – the Triple Crown triumph was a welcome return to form for skipper Katy McLean's side.

England kicked off against France in the Stade des Alpes in February and although two penalties from McLean gave the visitors a first-half lead, two second-half tries from hooker Gaelle Mignot were enough to seal an 18-6 win for the home side.

Eight days later England faced Scotland in Aberdeen and the side were simply unstoppable, running in 11 tries from 11 different players to set up a 63-0 success.

Ireland were the next opponents and after losing 25-0 to them the previous season, Street's team were looking for revenge. They got it at Twickenham with a 17-10 victory thanks to tries from number eight Sarah Hunter, wing Kay Wilson and flanker Marlie Packer.

Only Wales now stood in the way of England and the Triple Crown. The two teams faced each other at the Stoop in London but once Emily Scarratt had raced over for the first of her two tries, the game was over as a contest. Natasha Brennan scored on her debut, whilst Margaret Alphonsi and Wilson also crossed and England were convincing 35-3 winners.

"We set the target for the girls post-France to win four games and see what happens," Street said after wrapping up the Triple Crown. "I think we have learnt some good lessons from France. It's sharpened our minds up definitely and we said we needed to bounce back. The strength of a good side is not the defeats, it's what you do afterwards."

England had to beat the Italians and hope France lost their final match at home against Ireland to win the Six Nations. They won in Italy 20-0 with tries from Danielle Waterman, back in the team after 14 months out with a knee injury, Scarratt, winning her 50th cap, Laura Keates and Amber Reed but France held their nerve to beat the Irish 19-15 and claim the title.

The silverware was on its way to Paris rather than London but England's women could still look back on a Six Nations that was a springboard for their bid to win the World Cup staged in France later in the year.

FINAL TABLE

	W	D	L	T	F	A	Pts
France	5	0	0	25	162	21	10
England	4	0	1	23	145	31	8
Ireland	3	0	2	20	137	42	6
Italy	2	0	3	8	57	108	4
Wales	1	0	4	5	45	88	2
Scotland	0	0	5	1	5	261	0

ENGLAND MATCH STATS 2014

RBS 6 NATIONS

FRANCE 26 ENGLAND 24
Stade de France, 1 February

ENGLAND
Tries: Brown, Burell
Conversion: Farrell
Penalty Goals: Farrell (2), Goode
Drop Goal: Care

FRANCE:
Tries: Huget (2), Fickou
Conversion: Machenaud
Penalty Goals: Doussain, Machenaud (2)

SCOTLAND 0 ENGLAND 20
Murrayfield, 8 February

ENGLAND
Tries: Brown, Burrell
Conversions: Farrell (2)
Penalty Goal: Farrell
Drop Goal: Care

ENGLAND 13 IRELAND 10
Twickenham, 22 February

ENGLAND
Try: Care
Conversion: Farrell
Penalty Goals: Farrell (2)

IRELAND
Try: Kearney
Conversion: Sexton
Penalty Goal: Sexton

ENGLAND 29 WALES 18
Twickenham, 9 March

ENGLAND
Try: Burrell, Care
Conversions: Farrell (2)
Penalty Goals: Farrell (5)

WALES
Penalty Goals: Halfpenny (6)

ITALY 11 ENGLAND 52
Stadio Olimpico, 15 March

ENGLAND
Tries: Brown (2), Farrell, Nowell, Robshaw, Tuilagi, Vunipola
Conversions: Farrell (7)
Penalty Goal: Farrell

ITALY
Try: Sarto
Penalty Goals: Orquera

NEW ZEALAND TOUR

NEW ZEALAND 20 ENGLAND 15
Auckland, 7 June

ENGLAND
Penalty Goals: Burns (4), Cipriani

NEW ZEALAND
Try: C Smith
Penalty Goals: Cruden (5)

NEW ZEALAND 28 ENGLAND 27
Dunedin, 14 June

ENGLAND
Tries: Yarde, Brown, Ashton
Conversions: Farrell (3)
Penalty Goals: Farrell (2)

NEW ZEALAND
Tries: B Smith, Savea, Nonu
Conversions: Cruden, Barrett
Penalty Goals: Cruden (2), Barrett

NEW ZEALAND 36 ENGLAND 13
Hamilton, 21 June

ENGLAND
Try: Yarde
Conversion: Burns
Penalty Goals: Burns (2)

NEW ZEALAND
Tries: Savea (3), A Smith (2)
Conversions: Cruden (3), Barrett
Penalty Goal: Cruden

Ruckley's
Spot the Ball

Can you use your rugby knowledge to decide which is the real ball in the picture below?

Answer on Page 61

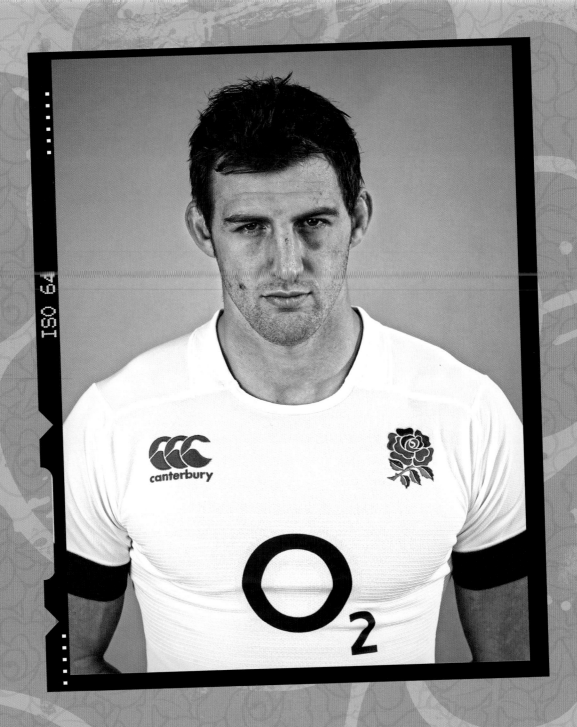

In The Spotlight

Back rowers have an amazing work rate but nobody works harder, puts in more tackles or covers more ground than the incredible Northampton Saints flanker.

Some players make the headlines with tries while others catch the eye with tackles. The kickers get noticed when they land a conversion, penalty or drop goal but Tom Wood's game is all about the hard work and without him in the pack, England would be a weaker team.

He was first drafted into the side in 2011 to face Wales in Cardiff and ever since his Test debut the Saints player has been the man who makes the England forwards tick. Injuries have disrupted his career but when fully fit, Wood is a world-class blind-side flanker.

He learnt his rugby at the Worcester Warriors Academy. A short spell playing in New Zealand for North Otago furthered his education and it wasn't long before he was in the Warriors first team. In 2010 he signed for Northampton and after impressing for the Saxons side the same year, he was ready for the Test team.

His great form for the Saints in the 2010-11 season was recognised when he was named the Premiership Player of the Season and he was at his brilliant best again in 2014 as Northampton were crowned league champions for the first time.

Wood frequently tops the tackle count for England in Test matches and he's a superb jumper at the back of the lineout. He can also play at number eight and is a natural leader who often captains the Saints.

The flanker was part of the England team that won the Six Nations title in 2011 but his greatest performance for his country came in 2012 when he was named Man of the Match after the team's dazzling 38-21 win over the All Blacks at Twickenham.

THAT'S A FACT!

The Saints flanker is a talented archer and when he lived in New Zealand he liked to hunt for wild deer with his bow and arrow.

ENGLAND UNDER-20S
RULE THE WORLD

After winning the IRB Junior World Championship for the first time in 2013, England's brilliant youngsters were crowned champions again after a dramatic victory over South Africa in the 2014 final in Auckland.

English rugby's future looks bright after the Under 20 team successfully defended their world title with a heroic 21-20 triumph over South Africa at Eden Park, the second time in 12 months the side lifted the prized trophy.

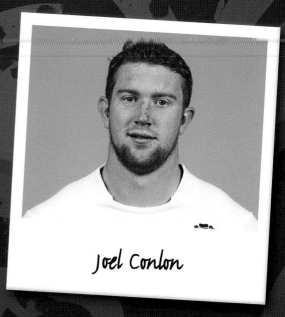

Joel Conlon

England kicked off their campaign in New Zealand with a thumping 63-3 defeat of Italy in Pukekohe which featured a hat-trick from Earle. They then beat Australia comfortably in Auckland but were made to work much harder in their final group game against Argentina, sealing victory with a late penalty from fly half Sam Olver.

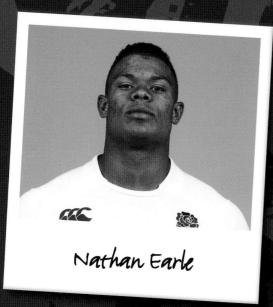

Nathan Earle

Nick Walshe's side became world champions for the first time after beating Wales 23-15 in the final in 2013 and thanks to tries from wing Nathan Earle and flanker Joel Conlon against the Baby Boks in 2014, England were able to celebrate another famous win.

"It doesn't feel real at the moment," said England captain Maro Itoje after beating the South Africans. "It feels pretty special. It's something I dreamt of and I am so happy to be able to lift the trophy. We believed if we stayed true to our principles, we would do well and we did. This has been a fantastic tournament for us. Our boys have worked so hard and we got our just deserts."

Sam Olver

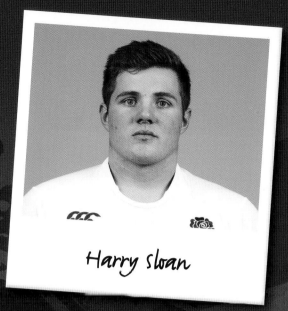

Harry Sloan

Danny Hobbs-Awoyemi

The result meant England finished top of Group A and faced Ireland in the semi-finals in Auckland. A try in the eighth minute from centre Harry Sloan gave Walshe's team a dream start and further first-half scores from prop Danny Hobbs-Awoyemi, wing Howard Packman and hooker Tom Woolstencroft saw England storm into a 34-3 lead at the break. Flanker Gus Jones added a fourth try in the second-half and the final score was 42-15 to the defending champions.

The final at Eden Park saw the junior Springboks race into an early lead with a try from centre Jessie Kriel but Earle's score just before half-time made it 11-10 to England and after Conlon went over in the 50th minute, the score was 21-13.

South Africa scored a second try through Kriel with 17 minutes left but despite a late onslaught, England's defence held firm and the trophy was theirs again.

"Any World Cup final win is tough and this is a magnificent effort and I am so unbelievably proud of the boys," said Walshe. "Last year it was special because it was the first, this year it is special because of where we are and what it means and how we have played. It's been phenomenal."

Howard Packman

Tom Woolstencroft

Gus Jones

ENGLAND'S ROUTE TO GLORY
Group A
England 63 Italy 3 (2 June, Pukekohe)
England 38 Australia 24 (6 June, Auckland)
England 17 Argentina 16 (10 June, Auckland)
Semi-Final
England 42 Ireland 15 (15 June, North Harbour)
Final
England 21 South Africa 20 (20 June, Auckland)

CAPTAIN FANTASTIC!

Tom Mitchell

England skipper Tom Mitchell finished the 2013-14 HSBC Sevens World Series as the tournament's top points scorer.

Captains are meant to lead by example and Tom Mitchell did just that for the England Sevens in the latest Sevens World Series, finishing the competition with an incredible 358 points from the nine events on the worldwide fixture list.

Mitchell's marvellous haul during the 2013-14 season included 32 tries and left him almost 100 points in front of the next player on the list, Fiji's Samisoni Viriviri.

It was also another brilliant year for the England speedster Dan Norton. He was the tournament's top try scorer in the 2012-13 season and his 27 tries in 2013-14 took his career tally in the Series to 164 and fifth on the all-time list of try scorers.

Inspired by Mitchell and Norton, England finished fourth in the World Series behind New Zealand, South Africa and Fiji, which compared to the team's sixth-place finish the year before and a strong debut season for new England head coach Simon Amor.

Dan Bibby

England began the Series in October by reaching the semi-finals of Gold Coast Sevens in Australia, undoing the Springboks 47-0 in their final match thanks to two tries each from Phil Burgess, James Rodwell and Dan Bibby to claim third place.

Phil Burgess

The side couldn't improve on that result until the Japan Sevens in Tokyo in March. There was heartbreak when Amor's side were beaten in the semi-finals by South Africa, but there was also celebration when they defeated defending champions New Zealand 21-12 in the third-place play-off match with tries from Jack Clifford, Bibby and Burgess.

England's best performance of the season came in the famous Hong Kong Sevens in March when they battled past South Africa and Fiji on the second day of action to reach the final. They faced New Zealand again but despite Tom Powell's converted try, this time it was the Kiwis who were the winners with a 26-7 victory.

"You get so few opportunities to play in front of 40,000 with an atmosphere as incredible as it is here and I thought the courage and the way the guys played for the shirt and their country, and really fought together throughout the weekend was just outstanding. It says so much about them as a group. We'll keep on building and hopefully next year we can go one stage further," he added.

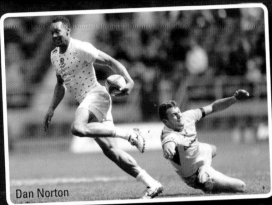
Dan Norton

Another third-place finish in their home event, the London Sevens at Twickenham, saw England end the Sevens World Series on a high and with Amor and his players improving all the time, expect a strong showing from the side in the 2014-15 tournament.

James Rodwell

In The Spotlight

Joe Launchbury

The dynamic Wasps second row has made a spectacular impact on the Test team since making his debut in 2012.

Since winning his first cap against Fiji at Twickenham, Joe Launchbury hasn't wasted any time in making a name for himself as one of the hottest young talents in world rugby.

The Wasps forward was only 21 when he came off the bench against the Fijians but since then he hasn't missed a single Test and he was voted Man of the Series after England's autumn internationals in 2012, which included the brilliant defeat of New Zealand at Twickenham.

His success has been built on his awesome power in the tight, his remarkable pace for a second row out wide and his reliability at the front of the lineout.

Launchbury's route to England recognition was not easy. He was a member of the Harlequins Academy as a teenager but when he was released by the club, he joined National League 2 South side Worthing. Test rugby seemed a distant dream but when he was spotted by scouts from Wasps in 2010, his career was about to get back on track.

He made his Premiership debut for the London club against Leicester in early 2011 and later in the same year he was part of the England Under 20 team that won the Six Nations Grand Slam. He quickly established himself as a first-choice selection under Lancaster in the senior side and in May 2013 he was named as the England Player of the Year for 2012-13 after only nine games.

It's been an amazing two years for Launchbury but the good news for England fans is that the best is yet to come from the young Wasps forward.

Courtney Lawes, England

THAT'S A FACT!

Joe's father Steve was a professional soldier who served with the Royal Marines for 27 years.

45

21 June – England's Manu Tuilagi (2nd L) tries to break through Jerome Kaino (L) and Sam Whitelock (2nd R)

ENGLAND IN NEW ZEALAND

Stuart Lancaster's side couldn't quite manage a famous win against the All Blacks in the summer of 2014 but they emerged from the three-Test series with their heads held high.

There's no tougher place to tour in world rugby than New Zealand. Few teams come away from playing the All Blacks in their own backyard with victory and in their 13 previous visits to the home of the reigning world champions, England had won only two Tests.

Lancaster's team of 2014 nearly beat the Kiwis twice and despite the disappointment of two dramatic near misses, England can reflect on a summer in which they proved they're getting stronger and stronger.

The first Test in Auckland in early June saw Lancaster forced to field what some people called an understrength side because the head coach couldn't pick any Northampton or Saracens players, but the 15 that started against the All Blacks at Eden Park were incredible.

The forwards in particular were superb and fly half Freddie Burns in great form with the boot, kicking four penalties. With just three minutes left to play, the score was level at 15-15. England was looking for victory but Conrad Smith squeezed over in the corner to give New Zealand a last-gasp 20-15 win.

"It was a fantastic effort and it's a shame we couldn't nail it," Lancaster said after the match. "We're tremendously proud of how they did and with the quality of players sat in the stand, it was tough on them not to come away with anything."

England regrouped for the second Test and with Lancaster now able to select the players fresh from Northampton's Premiership win over Saracens, it was a powerful side that lined up for the game in Dunedin.

They made a great start in the Forsyth Barr Stadium when Marland Yarde scored after only seven minutes and after an Owen Farrell penalty, England led 10-6 at half-time.

The All Blacks came roaring back into the game after the break with three tries in 20 minutes but England refused to collapse and late scores from Chris Ashton and Mike Brown changed the match. Farrell converted both tries but there just wasn't enough for the side to create the winning score and when the final whistle blew it was 28-27 to New Zealand.

21 June – Danny Cipriani (L) of England kicks the ball as New Zealand's All Black McCaw tries to block

14 June – New Zealand All Blacks' Conrad Smith and England's Mike Brown (R) talk after the second rugby union test match

21 June – New Zealand's All Blacks Malakai Fekitoa (L) is tackled by England's Tom Wood

"We've come a long way in the past few weeks and we'll continue to get better," insisted skipper Chris Robshaw. "We finished really strongly, we started really strongly, it was just that middle bit."

England's growing strength in depth was shown when the midweek side comfortably beat Super Rugby side the Crusaders 38-7 with tries from Joe Gray, Ben Foden, Brad Barritt, Alex Goode, Anthony Watson and Chris Pennell.

The third Test in Hamilton came four days later but it was a match too far after a long season, and although Yarde went over a second-half score that took his career tally to an impressive four tries in just five Tests, England fell to a 36-13 defeat.

It wasn't the fairytale end that England had hoped for but according to Lancaster, it was a tour that still had plenty of positives.

14 June – Marland Yarde celebrates

RED ROSES CROWNED WORLD CHAMPIONS

After three defeats in the three previous finals, England lifted the Women's World Cup for the first time in 20 years after a stunning 21-9 victory over Canada in Paris.

It was back in 1994 that England's women last proudly held the World Cup. Since then they had reached three more finals but each time they came up against New Zealand and although they were never beaten by more than 10 points, each time the Red Roses left empty handed.

It was a heartbreaking run of results but the smiles were finally back in 2014 as Gary Street's brilliant side put all those disappointments behind them to overcome Canada in a thrilling final and earn the title of world champions again.

England scored two tries in the final in the Stade Jean Bouin with full-back Danielle Waterman going over in the first half in France and centre Emily Scarratt racing over for a superb solo effort after the break. A conversion and three penalties from Scarratt completed the scoring and although Magali Harvey kicked three penalties for the Canadians, England ran out 21-9 winners.

"We've worked so hard for this and there are so many great legends that have gone before us that haven't won in an England shirt," said England captain Katy McLean after the match. "That's for all of them who are here today. It started years ago with the people that have brought us here, our family and friends. We've had to work today - Canada were fantastic - and it's amazing to think we've done it."

England were drawn in the same group as Canada, Samoa and Spain and began the tournament in incredible form, scoring 10 tries in a 65-3 demolition of the Samoans. Four days later they faced Spain and Street's team were again unstoppable as they scored six tries, including a double from flanker Marlie Packer, to record an impressive 45-5 victory.

The final group game was the big one against Canada and it was tense and tight. England trailed to an early Canadian try but hit back with a five-pointer from number eight Sarah Hunter in the second half. Canada were 13-10 behind with just seven minutes left but a late penalty saw the match finish 13-13.

The result saw England top the group but Canada also progressed to the knockout stages as the best runners-up.

Ireland stood in England's way in the semi-final but the Red Roses' place in the final was never in doubt. Prop Rochelle Clark began the scoring with a 25th minute try while Packer scored another brilliant double from the bench and England were celebrating a convincing 40-7 win.

If England were nervous going into the final for their rematch with Canada, they didn't show it and two early penalties from Scarratt eased the team into a 6-0 lead. Waterman's try seven minutes from half time was a fabulous team score and at the break the Red Roses had an 11-3 cushion.

Two penalties from Harvey made it 11-9 but Scarratt, who finished as the tournament's top points scorer, made sure there was no late Canadian fightback with her amazing 75th minute try, powering her way through four tackles to make sure England got their hands on the World Cup for the first time since 1994.

"It's a pretty amazing feeling and I am just so proud of everyone involved," said coach Street. "It's a really special group. We've been on a long journey but to have that trophy makes it worthwhile."

DID YOU KNOW? PLAYER TRIVIA

England skipper **CHRIS ROBSHAW** has taught himself to juggle to help him improve his hand-eye co-ordination.

Scrum half **LEE DICKSO**N is hooked on footwear and has more than 50 pairs of trainers.

He's only five foot eight tall but winger **CHRISTIAN WADE** played basketball for the South of England as a kid and dreamed of a career in the NBA in America.

Winger **MARLAND YARDE** could have been a footballer and was part of the QPR Academy when he was a teenager.

Centre **MANU TUIGALI** can complete the Rubik's Cube in just two minutes.

Hooker **TOM YOUNGS** is a part-time farmer and has a collection of model tractors.

ALEX CORBISIERO is nicknamed the 'hip-hop prop' after rapping a song during his England initiation.

Back rower **BILLY VUNIPOLA** entertains the England squad by singing Tina Turner songs on the team bus.

Winger **JACK NOWELL** is terrified of snakes after his own pet snake wrapped itself around his neck when he was a child.

Fly half **FREDDIE BURNS** has a fake zebra hanging on the wall of his flat.

Ruckley's
England Quiz

Are you England rugby's ultimate fan? Test your knowledge with our brilliant quiz.

All the answers can be found somewhere in the annual.

1 What was the score when England beat Wales at Twickenham in the Six Nations to win the Triple Crown?

2 Which England star can complete the Rubik's Cube in only 2 minutes?

3 Who is the coach of the England women's team?

4 Against which side did England captain Chris Robshaw make his international debut?

5 With which club did Stuart Lancaster start his coaching career?

6 Who has scored the most points in Test matches for England?

7 Who did the England Under 20 team beat in the final of the 2014 Junior World Championship?

8 In what year did England win the World Cup?

9 Which England player is scared of snakes?

10 Which England star was the top points scorer in the 2013-14 Sevens World Series?

11 England assistant coach Andy Farrell used to play rugby league for which club?

12 How many matches will Twickenham host during the 2015 World Cup?

13 What's the capacity of Twickenham?

14 Which new boy scored three tries in his first four England games during the 2014 Six Nations?

15 England flanker Tom Wood used to go hunting with what weapon?

16 Who is the most capped player in the history of English rugby?

17 Who scored England's only try in their 13-10 win against Ireland in the Six Nations?

18 Who is the England forwards coach?

19 How many teams will be playing at the 2015 World Cup?

20 Who was voted England Player of the Year for the 2012-13 season?

Answers on Page 61

ENGLAND RUGBY

ALEX CORBISIERO

Club: Northampton Saints
Height: 1.86m
Debut: v Italy (12/2/11)
Points: 0

Position: Prop
Weight: 118kg
Caps: 19

ALEX GOODE

Club: Saracens
Height: 1.81m
Debut: v South Africa (16/6/12)
Points: 3(1PG)

Position: Full back
Weight: 85kg
Caps: 16

ANTHONY WATSON

Club: Bath Rugby
Height: 1.90m
Debut: Uncapped
Points: 0

Position: Wing / Full back
Weight: 98kg
Caps: 0

BEN FODEN

Club: Northampton Saints
Height: 1.83m
Debut: v Italy (7/2/09)
Points: 35 (7T)

Position: Wing / Full back
Weight: 93kg
Caps: 34

BEN MORGAN

Club: Gloucester Rugby
Height: 1.91m
Debut: v Scotland (4/2/12)
Points: 10 (2T)

Position: No.8
Weight: 116kg
Caps: 23

PLAYER PROFILES

BEN YOUNGS

Club: Leicester Tigers
Height: 1.78m
Debut: v Scotland (13/3/10)
Points: 00 (0T)

Position: Scrum half
Weight: 92kg
Caps: 38

BILL TWELVETREES

Club: Gloucester Rugby
Height: 1.91m
Debut: v Scotland (2/2/13)
Points: 15 (3T)

Position: Fly half / Centre
Weight: 100kg
Caps: 14

BILLY VUNIPOLA

Club: Saracens
Height: 1.88m
Debut: v Argentina (8/6/13)
Points: 5 (1T)

Position: Flanker / No.8
Weight: 126kg
Caps: 10

BRAD BARRITT

Club: Saracens
Height: 1.86m
Debut: v Scotland (4/2/12)
Points: 5 (1T)

Position: Centre
Weight: 95kg
Caps: 18

CHRIS ASHTON

Club: Saracens
Height: 1.83m
Debut: v France (20/3/10)
Points: 95 (19T)

Position: Wing
Weight: 92kg
Caps: 39

ENGLAND RUGBY

CHRIS ROBSHAW

Club: Harlequins
Height: 1.88m
Debut: v Argentina (13/6/09)
Points: 10 (2T)

Position: Back row
Weight: 110kg
Caps: 28

CHRISTIAN WADE

Club: London Wasps
Height: 1.78m
Debut: v Argentina (8/6/13)
Points: 0

Position: Wing
Weight: 86kg
Caps: 1

COURTNEY LAWES

Club: Northampton Saints
Height: 2.00m
Debut: v Australia (7/11/09)
Points: 0

Position: Lock / Flanker
Weight: 111kg
Caps: 32

DAN COLE

Club: Leicester Tigers
Height: 1.89m
Debut: v Wales (6/2/10)
Points: 5 (1T)

Position: Prop
Weight: 118kg
Caps: 45

DANNY CARE

Club: Harlequins
Height: 1.74m
Debut: v New Zealand (14/6/08)
Points: 44 (7T, 3DG)

Position: Scrum half
Weight: 85kg
Caps: 48

PLAYER PROFILES

DAVID ATTWOOD

Club: Bath Rugby
Height: 2.01m
Debut: v New Zealand (6/11/10)
Points: 0

Position: Lock
Weight: 118kg
Caps: 12

DAVID WILSON

Club: Bath Rugby
Height: 1.87m
Debut: v Argentina (6/6/09)
Points: 0

Position: Prop
Weight: 112kg
Caps: 37

DYLAN HARTLEY

Club: Northampton Saints
Height: 1.85m
Debut: v Pacific Islanders (8/11/08)
Points: 5 (1T)

Position: Hooker
Weight: 110kg
Caps: 57

ED SLATER

Club: Leicester Tigers
Height: 1.98m
Debut: Uncapped
Points: 0

Position: Lock / Back row
Weight: 116kg
Caps: 0

FREDDIE BURNS

Club: Leicester Tigers
Height: 1.88m
Debut: v New Zealand (1/12/12)
Points: 57 (1T, 8C, 12PG)

Position: Fly half
Weight: 88kg
Caps: 5

ENGLAND RUGBY

GEOFF PARLING

Club: Leicester Tigers
Height: 1.98m
Debut: v Scotland (4/2/12)
Points: 5 (1T)

Position: Lock / Flanker
Weight: 114kg
Caps: 21

GEORGE FORD

Club: Bath Rugby
Height: 1.75m
Debut: v Wales (9/3/14)
Points: 0

Position: Fly half
Weight: 84kg
Caps: 2

HENRY THOMAS*

Club: Sale Sharks
Height: 1.85m
Debut: v Argentina (8/6/13)
Points: 0

Position: Prop
Weight: 111kg
Caps: 7

JACK NOWELL*

Club: Exeter Chiefs
Height: 1.80m
Debut: v France (1/2/14)
Points: 5 (1T)

Position: Wing
Weight: 89kg
Caps: 5

JOE LAUNCHBURY

Club: London Wasps
Height: 1.98m
Debut: v Fiji (10/11/12)
Points: 10 (2T)

Position: Lock
Weight: 115kg
Caps: 22

PLAYER PROFILES

JOE MARLER

Club: Harlequins
Height: 1.84m
Debut: v South Africa (9/6/12)
Points: 0

Position: Prop
Weight: 118kg
Caps: 22

JONNY MAY*

Club: Gloucester Rugby
Height: 1.86m
Debut: v Argentina (15/6/13)
Points: 0

Position: Wing
Weight: 90kg
Caps: 7

KYLE EASTMOND

Club: Bath Rugby
Height: 1.71m
Debut: v Argentina (8/6/13)
Points: 5 (1T)

Position: Centre
Weight: 80kg
Caps: 4

LEE DICKSON

Club: Northampton Saints
Height: 1.78m
Debut: v Scotland (4/2/12)
Points: 0

Position: Scrum half
Weight: 85kg
Caps: 18

LUTHER BURRELL*

Club: Northampton Saints
Height: 1.91m
Debut: v France (1/2/14)
Points: 15 (3T)

Position: Centre
Weight: 109kg
Caps: 7

ENGLAND RUGBY

MATTHEW MULLAN*

Club: London Wasps
Height: 1.83m
Debut: v Italy (14/2/10)
Points: 0

Position: Prop
Weight: 112kg
Caps: 5

MAKO VUNIPOLA

Club: Saracens
Height: 1.80m
Debut: v Fiji (10/11/12)
Points: 5 (1T)

Position: Prop
Weight: 130kg
Caps: 15

MANUSAMOA TUILAGI

Club: Leicester Tigers
Height: 1.85m
Debut: v Wales (6/8/11)
Points: 55 (11T)

Position: Centre
Weight: 112kg
Caps: 25

MARLAND YARDE

Club: Harlequins
Height: 1.83m
Debut: v Argentina (15/6/13)
Points: 20 (4T)

Position: Wing
Weight: 95kg
Caps: 5

MATT KVESIC

Club: Gloucester Rugby
Height: 1.86m
Debut: v Argentina (8/6/13)
Points: 0

Position: Flanker
Weight: 104kg
Caps: 2

PLAYER PROFILES

MIKE BROWN

Club: Harlequins
Height: 1.83m
Debut: v South Africa (26/5/07)
Points: 25 (5T)
Position: Full back
Weight: 89kg
Caps: 29

OWEN FARRELL

Club: Saracens
Height: 1.88m
Debut: v Scotland (4/2/12)
Points: 271 (2T, 33C, 64P, 1DG)
Position: Fly half
Weight: 96kg
Caps: 25

ROB WEBSTER*

Club: Bath Rugby
Height: 1.83m
Debut: v Italy (11/2/12)
Points: 5 (1T)
Position: Hooker
Weight: 110kg
Caps: 8

TOM WOOD

Club: Northampton Saints
Height: 1.95m
Debut: v Wales (4/2/11)
Points: 0
Position: Flanker
Weight: 109kg
Caps: 30

TOM YOUNGS

Club: Leicester Tigers
Height: 1.75m
Debut: v Fiji (10/11/12)
Points: 0
Position: Hooker
Weight: 102kg
Caps: 17

* England Saxons squad – players capped for elite team in 2013/14 season.

England Rugby

MIKE BROWN

Ruckley's
Quiz Answers

Guess Who?, Page 27

1: Marler 2: Foden 3: Wilson 4: Vunipola

Spot the Ball, Page 37

England Quiz, Page 51

1	29-18	8	2003	15	Bow and arrow
2	Manu Tuilagi	9	Jack Nowell	16	Jason Leonard
3	Gary Street	10	Tom Mitchell	17	Danny Care
4	Argentina	11	Wigan Warriors	18	Graham Rowntree
5	Leeds	12	10	19	20
6	Jonny Wilkinson	13	82,000	20	Joe Launchbury
7	South Africa	14	Luther Burrell